**W9-BEM-562**

STOP THE LIES

Exposing the Evils of Abortion
to the Next Generation

America Needs Fatima's
Hope for the Unborn Campaign

STOP THE LIES

Exposing the Evils of Abortion
to the Next Generation

America Needs Fatima
P.O. Box 341, Hanover, PA 17331
(888) 317-5571
ANF@ANF.org • www.ANF.org

Copyright © 2017. The American Society for the Defense of Tradition, Family and Property®—TFP® and it's *America Needs Fatima* campaign.

All rights reserved. No part of this publication may be reproduced, stored in a retrieval system, or transmitted, in any form or by any means, electronic or mechanical, including photocopying, recording or any information storage and retrieval system, without prior written permission from The American Society for the Defense of Tradition, Family and Property®—TFP®.

The American Society for the Defense of Tradition, Family and Property® and TFP® are registered names of the Foundation for a Christian Civilization, Inc., a 501(c)(3) tax-exempt organization.

Cover/book design: Elizabeth Saracino
Cover Photo: © Derektenhue | Dreamstime

The current publication is a reprint of the 1992 book entitled "The Womb Becomes a Tomb".
Statistical data referenced in the original has been retained with the exception of the latest available figures for the number of abortions in the United States.

ISBN: 978-1-877905-50-6
Library of Congress Control Number: 2017961781

Printed in the United States of America

— CONTENTS —

Moloch Resurrected in Our Own Times

Moloch was a god of the ancient Canaanites, or Phoenicians. He was considered a symbol of the purifying fire, which, in turn, was the symbol of the spirit. As a result of a catastrophe at the beginning of time, this spirit transformed itself into darkness by becoming matter.

According to the Phoenician beliefs, men were the incarnation of this ontogenetic tragedy. To be redeemed from this sin, it was necessary to offer human sacrifice to Moloch by immolating their little children, because they were the most permeated with matter.

Throwing firstborn infants into the fire to free them from matter constituted the most agreeable sacrifice that could be offered to that implacable divinity, represented as a gigantic bronze statue whose cavernous body contained a furnace. Mothers threw their own live children into the incandescent belly of Moloch who, waiting with open arms, devoured his poor little victims in the flames.

In order not to cause repugnance among those attending this scene, the iniquitous priests of Moloch took care to have trumpets sound and drums beat to drown out the infernal music of the cries of the innocent.[1]

With neither pity nor piety thousands of children were immolated by the pagan Phoenicians.

But only by them?

In our own times, the self-designated era of human rights, something similar is happening.

Though there be no more Phoenician priests, their place

has been taken by unscrupulous doctors. The belly of Moloch has given place to the mother's womb. The womb has become a tomb.

To what god are these millions of innocent victims offered in holocaust?

The modern gods vary according to a macabre polytheism:

Eros, that is, the dominant cult of pleasure and the transformation of sex into a commercial product that must not cause the slightest inconvenience to the consumer. Abortion is the ultimate guarantee that Eros can be worshipped without bother.

Ego, that is, the tyrannical self-interest of parents who, for mere personal convenience, eliminate a child as casually as they would remove a pimple from their face.

Leviathan, that is, the hypocritical state that speaks so much about human rights and tolerates not the least form of racial or social discrimination, but that nevertheless crosses its arms in face of this most clamorous injustice, the extermination of its unborn, the most helpless of beings. Does it not know that the most elementary of human rights is the right to life? And that the most odious form of discrimination is that based on the victim's stage of physical development, that is, his age?

But the modern Moloch is much more implacable than the Canaanite god. Indeed, if you compare the fifty-eight million American children sacrificed in the womb,* in the silence of cold operating rooms, the human sacrifices of antiquity seem almost ridiculous.

The paradox could not be more flagrant: the mother, the doctors, and the public authorities are precisely those from whom the unborn should most expect to find care and protection.

The mother, to whom a child turns to find love, instead immolates him, not on an altar, but on an operating table. The doctor, who should work to safeguard his life, is the cause of his death. The state, advancing its agenda of birth control, denies him the right to life.

A tragic symbol of the moral decadence of our society, abortion is also a sign of its profound dehumanization and irrationality. It is dehumanizing because of the trivial consideration it gives human life, as if it were a breeze without a specific finality and without a transcendent destiny. As a result we see that "the humanicide generation cannot hope for *humaneness* in the generation to which it gives birth, because children are not customarily more generous and dedicated than their parents. The coin with which the children of the humanicide generation will repay them is massive euthanasia."[2]

Not only is it irrational to kill an innocent human being, but it is also something that profoundly contradicts human nature. It is a fundamental disorder which distances us from the most basic moral principle that commands us to respect the life of those similar to us.

Good and evil, justice and injustice are not mere conven-

---

* The number of abortions in America as of January 14, 2016 was a staggering 58,586,256 as reported by LifeNews.com. (Information retrieved at http://www.lifenews.com/2016/01/14/58586256-abortions-in-america-since-roe-v-wade-in-1973/ on November 20, 2017.)

tions, nor just the whim of men. Rather, they are the adequation of our personal conduct in relation to our duties.

As Josef Pieper pointed out so well:

> **We must learn to experience as reality the knowledge that the establishment of right and justice has not received its fullest and most valid legitimation until we have gone back to the absolute foundation; and that there is no other way to make the demands of justice effective as absolute bounds set the will to power.**

> **This means in concrete terms: Man has inalienable rights because he is created a person by the act of God, that is, an act beyond all human discussion. In the ultimate analysis, then, something is inalienably due to man because he is *creatura*. Moreover, as *creatura*, man has the absolute duty to give another his due.[3]**

Be a Mother, Not a Molochite

History repeats itself. Just as Canaanite mothers were fooled by iniquitous priests into sacrificing to the idol Moloch, we can see that there are many women today who, fooled by the sophisms of the perverse proponents of abortion, are induced into becoming modern worshipers of Moloch. We hope that sound arguments may yet save some of them, before their tender motherly hearts harden completely and become hearts of bronze, from committing such a hateful crime that cries out to heaven for vengeance. It is with this intention that America Needs Fatima publishes this work, hoping thereby to make a modest contribution to the magnificent apostolate that dedicated pro-lifers and pro-life organizations have been carrying on for so long.

Awaiting Death

In the waiting room of a clinic, four women anxiously await the nurse's call. Tense and with somber expressions, they neither speak among themselves nor glance at one another. Some smoke incessantly.

The tension contrasts with the tranquility the decor tries to induce: rose-colored walls with small paintings depicting scenes of nature exuberant with life; pleasant and soothing music; everything clean and well arranged.

The frozen smile of the nurse complements the sterile whiteness of her uniform and the subtle odor of antiseptic which permeates the place.

A syrupy voice calls one of the clients. She appears to be about twenty and is far along in her pregnancy.

Nervously putting out her cigarette, she waveringly enters a long neon-lit corridor. The odor of ether is suffocating.

As she walks along, beads of cold sweat run down her face, and a sense of anguish pervades her. The echo of her slow and indecisive steps, growing louder and louder, is suddenly drowned out by the shrill noise of a motor emanating from one of the rooms she passes. The sound is vaguely reminiscent of a vacuum cleaner.

"Go in, dear," says the nurse, opening the door of the examination room.

Receiving the patient with a crocodile smile, the doctor tells her to take a seat.

"You're in luck, missy," the doctor says with a nasal voice, "you haven't been pregnant more than 19 weeks. If we do it right away, you'll save money. Besides, it will be easier all around," he concluded with the same simpering smile.

"What's going to happen, doctor? What will happen after the surgery?" the patient asks.

"I'm only going to extract a little fluid and replace it with another. You'll feel a few cramps and . . . everything will be okay. It didn't take much to get pregnant; it won't take much to undo it," remarks the surgeon cynically.

"Is there any danger?"

"No, it's simple procedure."

The Methods of Extermination

The syringe the abortionist uses to extract the fluid has an enormous four-inch needle. With it, he pierces the mother's abdominal wall and the amniotic sac where the baby is found. Sixty cc of amniotic fluid are removed, and then 200 cc of a strong saline solution are injected in its stead.

Immediately, that little being, who already has all his organs and even his fingerprints, begins to suffer violent convulsions.

Accustomed to the pleasant and beneficial swallows of the amniotic fluid in which he is immersed, he now experiences the bitter taste of a fatal poison. The caustic salt burns his throat, his delicate skin, his eyes yet to see the brilliance of the sun, his ears never to hear the sweet song of the birds. In vain, he tries to escape, throwing himself from side to side in terrible contortions.

The child's agony may last for hours. The mother can follow the slow torment of her child by his brusque movements of self-defense, which are as useless as they are desperate.

When death finally ensues, the tragic drama does not end. Several hours will still pass before the child, seared as the victim of a napalm attack, is expelled from the maternal cloister. So red is his scalded body that abortionists describe it as the "candy apple" effect.

But scientific methods of exterminating pre-born children are not limited to salt poisoning. The lethal "menu" varies greatly, depending on the period of gestation. Within the first three months of embryonic development, by which time all the necessary organs have already been formed and the heart has been beating for some time, the murder machine of choice is the vacuum aspirator.

Twenty-nine times more powerful than a household vacuum cleaner, this brutal mechanism of destruction uses a special tube to suck out the baby, tearing him with extreme violence from the walls of the uterus. Death comes within minutes, brought about by the total dismembering of the child.

In this grisly but profitable "business," methods of human extinction continually progress. Benefiting from enormous state subsidies, a network of exterminative entrepreneurs do everything possible to eliminate the slightest chances of survival of an unwanted child. Some children have survived "incomplete abortions" such as the little girl born in New York City minus an arm that was taken by the abortionist.

To facilitate the process of the suction of the fetus, the "humanicides" invented a new technique. Known as D&C (dilation and curettage), it consists in cutting the placenta and slicing up the body of the baby within the uterus before sucking it out. Special instruments called curettes are used for this purpose.

This method requires careful follow-up. The body of the unborn child, having been torn apart, has to be carefully put back together, piece by piece, before going into the garbage, sink, or incinerator to make sure that no piece is forgotten inside the womb. Otherwise, life-threatening infections could result for the mother.

If the child is more than twelve weeks old, D&E (dilation and evacuation) is used. By this time the baby's bones are already calcified and, therefore, use of a curette does not guarantee a successful operation. In this case, tongs are necessary for separating the bones, first of the legs and arms, then of the back; finally the head must be crushed before being sucked out. All of this without anesthetic, of course, since medical science notwithstanding, abortionists must deny that preborn babies can feel pain.

Finally, there remain two equally macabre methods of extermination: One uses the drug prostaglandin to induce premature delivery; the other, hysterotomy, is really nothing more than a caesarean procedure aimed not at saving the child but rather at killing it.

In these cases, the baby is killed outside the womb. Some

doctors use the placenta itself to smother the infant. However, there have been cases in which the necessary "care" was not taken, so that babies aborted by these methods have been found still alive in garbage bags.

Has Moral Sense Been Lost? And the Light of Reason?

These standard methods of abortion are widely known, having been photographed, filmed, and displayed in print and electronic media. Pro-life educational materials have made meritorious use of similar subject matter to sensitize the public to the slaughter of the unborn.

Nonetheless, in light of the rising number of induced abortions in the United States and around the world, several questions arise:[4]

- Do the horrible scenes of aborted babies at the most varied stages of gestation really affect the consciences of pro-abortionists in any way? Or do they at least help "indecisive" mothers choose life instead of death?

- Could large sectors of American public opinion already be in such a state of moral numbness that even such a bloodbath does not speak to their consciences anymore?

- What is the root cause of this moral insensibility to this most fundamental of human rights— the right to life?

- How can human flesh continue to be "sold and commercialized," often with government funds, in these modern "slaughterhouses?"

- Do not the more than 58,586,256 unborn babies murdered by abortion since *Roe v. Wade* constitute an American abortion holocaust?

Man is a being who is one and indivisible. Between his way of behaving and thinking there should be a strict correlation. For this reason, those who show themselves insensible to this slaughter of the innocents or who openly favor it, seek to justify this way of acting through psychological, doctrinal, biological, socioeconomic, and other rationalizations.

Scandalously, there are even attempts to find "religious"

The first step in abortion: inject a moral numbness, an "anesthetizing" amorality of consciences.

motives to make such nefarious crimes appear "reasonable" (in the etymological sense of the word).

What are the pretexts which serve to "anesthetize" these consciences?

To analyze each in depth would go beyond the scope of this work. We shall consider the most frequent ones in their fundamental aspects, showing their inherent inconsistency. This will leave us with even more ominous questions:

- Why, in face of the knowledge that the alleged justifications for abortions are vain, does this slaughter of the innocents grow every day with increasing fury?

- Could it be that *humanity* has become "*humanicide*"?[5] Could it be that it has lost the *lumen rationis*, the light of reason, which says to men that they should practice good and avoid evil?

Saint Thomas Aquinas explains the role of the principle of contradiction which he defines as the first and supreme principle of thinking, whereby man is capable of knowing and thinking. Without it, we would not be able to distinguish between what is and what is not. We would not be able to distinguish between truth and error, good and evil, beauty and ugliness. Everything would be confused; we would sink into the worst of absurdities.

A Fetus Is Not a Human Being?

When does human life begin? This is one of the central questions in the controversy about abortion. Pro-lifers and pro-abortionists disagree as to the answer, but agree that it is a key problem.

Many protagonists of abortion would have us believe that there are no victims, that nothing is being aborted. But the most elementary logic indicates that it is unnecessary to suppress nothing. As one pro-life bumper sticker proclaims, "If it is not alive, why kill it?"

If the fetus were simply a mass of undefined protoplasm, one might find a "reasonableness" in procured abortion. Extirpating a mere agglomeration of flesh could not be considered a crime; in certain cases it could even be considered healthy. There can be no homicide where there is no human life.

One could also then understand the "wisdom" of the U.S. Supreme Court's decision in 1973, when Associate Justice Harry Blackmun, writing for the majority, found that: "The word 'person,' as used in the Fourteenth Amendment, does not include the unborn."[6] (Ironically, that same Court has encountered no difficulties in attributing legal personhood to lakes, rivers, and forests.[7])

The allegation that a fetus is not a human being constitutes the basis of the "pro-choice" public argument. As the abortionist Dr. Martti Kekomaki cynically declared, "an aborted baby is just garbage."[8] Today the unborn are considered sub-human, as slaves were considered "things"[9] in the nineteenth century, and Jews under the Nazis.[10] The common denomina-

tor of these aberrations is the despotic discrimination which denies the humanity of its targets.

If the fetus is a human being, individual, autonomous and unrepeatable, procured abortion and homicide are identical. The unborn deserves the same legal protection that is the right of every man, since his life is as human as that of a child already born or that of any adult.

The problem, therefore, is to know whether the organism created at conception constitutes a human life. Since biology is the science of life, it is to the biologist, and not to the lawyer nor to the philosopher, that we must turn to ask:

- Is what is developing in the womb a human life?

- From what moment can we affirm that a new human life exists?

The First Instant

Life never begins. It is only transmitted. Living beings only come from other living beings. "In human reproduction, biological life does not begin: it is continuous. There is no period where life stops and later starts up again. Cells come only from living cells."[11]

This basic postulate of modern biology, applied to our case, proves that the rise of a new human being—human ontogeny—

is contained in the male and female gametes (sperm and egg, respectively) and is produced by the fusion of these two gametes. That is, through the fertilization of the egg by the sperm, a new cell, a zygote, is produced, having its own genetic code strictly distinct from that of the gametes whose fusion was the cause of its origin.

The fertilization of the egg by the sperm takes place in the fallopian tubes twelve to twenty-four hours after ovulation. As the zygote continues moving down the fallopian tube toward the uterus, the process of cell multiplication is already well under way. About six days after fertilization, the embryo begins to implant itself in the mucous membrane, the endometrium, of the uterus, at which point it begins to be called a blastocyst.

It is important to note that after this *first instant*, that is, after the fertilization of the egg, there is no other phase or stage in which the embryo receives a new or essential ontogenetic contribution in order for it to be what it is.

Thus, from this moment of fertilization, we have a new human life. As Dr. Jerome Lejeune, renowned French geneticist and discoverer of the cause of Down's Syndrome (Mongolism), summarized very well, "As soon as he has been conceived, a man is a man."[12]

From the first instant, the zygote is already a new human being.

Although the zygote is the result of the fusion of the gametes, there is an essential difference between them. The sperm and egg both contribute twenty-three chromosomes to form the zygote. This results, however, not in the simple biological addition of the sperm and egg, but gives rise to a strictly different and original being from the first instant.

The sperm cell contains a part of the genetic code of the father, the same code contained in every other cell of the father's body. In this sense it is part of his body. It is, furthermore, an adult cell, that is, one that has reached the full development necessary for achieving its reason for being, which is fertilization. If it does not fertilize an egg, there is no other alternative for it but death.

For its part, the egg contains a part of the genetic code of the mother and is also an adult cell that dies if it is not fertilized.

However, when the two gametes unite to form a zygote, that zygote contains a totally different and invariable genetic code. The zygote is neither a cell of the father nor of the mother. It possesses its own unrepeatable genetic message. **There never existed and will never exist again in history a being identical to this one.**

From the moment of fertilization, embryonic development continues in a linear way without undergoing any further genetic change. The embryo requires only time, nourishment, and oxygen to reach the full maturity of an adult person.

The zygote is not, therefore, a part of the mother or father. Far from being a simple adult cell, it is, rather, a cell which contains within itself an entire future of vital development.[13]

A Being Distinct from the Mother

The human embryo possesses a structure that is more complex than that of a newborn child, having a set of ancillary parts that are used only while in the uterus: the amniotic sac, the umbilical cord, and the placenta.

It is important to note that all of these auxiliary organs are not developed by the body of the mother, but by the fetus itself. They are parts of the new being and not parts of the mother.

In biological and genetic terms, it is not the mother who transforms her cells into the cells of the new being. It is the embryo which undertakes, in a veritable explosion of vitality, this "self-construction" within the habitat of the mother.

Describing this intra-uterine phase of life, Dr. William A. Liley, known as the "Father of Fetology," wrote:

. . . the young individual, in command of his environment and destiny with a tenacious purpose, implants in the spongy lining and with a display of physiological power, suppresses his mother's menstrual

From the first moment of conception, the embryo is a being distinct from the mother.

period. This is his home for the next 270 days and to make it habitable, the embryo develops a placenta and a protective capsule of fluid for himself. He also solves, single-handed, the homograft problem, that dazzling feat by which foetus and mother, although immunological foreigners who could not exchange skin grafts nor safely receive blood from each other, nevertheless tolerate each other in parabiosis for nine months.

We know that he moves with a delightful easy grace in his buoyant world, that foetal comfort determines foetal position. He is responsive to pain and touch and cold and sound and light. He drinks his amniotic fluid, more if it is artificially sweetened, less if it is given an unpleasant taste. He gets hiccups and sucks his thumb. He wakes and sleeps. He gets bored with repetitive signals but can be taught to be alerted by a first signal for a second different one. And, finally, he determines his birthday, for unquestionably, the onset of labour is a unilateral decision of the foetus.

This, then, is the foetus we know and, indeed, we each once were. This is the foetus we look after in modern obstetrics, the same baby we are caring for before and after birth, who before birth can be ill and need diagnosis and treatment just like any other patient.[14]

Is It a Man-Made Plan?

Based on these biological facts, it would be incorrect to say that the life of the child comes forth from the fetus, the embryo, or the zygote. The life of the zygote is just as human as that of an aged person, because it is the same life along the diverse stages of its development: embryonic, fetal, infantile, juvenile, pubescent, adult, and aged.

In the same way, one cannot speak of a "human plan," as a plan for a house, for example, is not the house itself. The zygote is already a human life, albeit only in its embryonic stage. Destroying the plans for, say, a $50,000 house, is not the same as destroying the edifice itself. On the contrary, the suppression of the life of a zygote is the suppression of a determinate human life.

> **[Consequently,] from the moment of conception, the life of every human being is to be respected in an absolute way because man is the only creature on earth that God has 'wished for Himself' and the spiritual soul of each man is 'immediately created' by God; his whole being bears the image of the Creator. Human life is sacred because from its beginning it involves 'the creative action of God,' and it remains forever in a special relationship with the Creator, Who is its sole end. God alone is the Lord of life from its beginning until its end: No one can in any circumstance claim for himself the right to destroy directly an innocent human being.[15]**

But It Does Not Even Look Human!

Someone, objecting, could ask: How is it possible for a human being to exist in something so minuscule and so lacking in even the slightest appearance of a human being?

The stages of human development cannot be compared to the steps involved in building an automobile on an assembly line, for example. The automobile exists only at the end of the assembly line when it has all the conditions for full operation.

If this analogy were valid for men, we would be forced to conclude that human life begins only at forty years of age, when men generally reach the fullness of maturity.

The myth of considering a being as human only by the physical characteristics that are visible after birth is scientifically and rationally unsustainable. Science conclusively proves that the human life at the moment of conception is the same, and no other, throughout the entire existence of a man.

Moreover, if we were to limit ourselves to considering simply the physical appearances, we would be unable to regard the newborn baby as human, since it does not yet have the characteristics of an adult.

We should, therefore, rely on the eyes of our intelligence, which tell us that a human individuality exists in the zygote.

Reality Versus the Law
Fertilization initiates a new human life that is both one and unique: one, because it is totally the same throughout every stage of its development; and unique, since it cannot be substituted for any other, possessing as it does characteristics which distinguish it from any other living being.

This biological reality precedes any philosophical or legal consideration. In other words, the law cannot *create* a human life nor decree the resurrection of a dead person. The law should limit itself to recognizing the reality of life and death.

To ascertain whether there be life or death, the lawmaker should have recourse to the biologist and doctor, never the contrary.

But is this what we find in regard to abortion?

In the famous *Roe v. Wade* decision of 1973, the Supreme Court departed from reality to embrace legal fiction, in denying the fact that human life begins at the moment of conception.

> **The Supreme Court effectively denied the "well-known facts of fetal development"** (*Wade*, p. 41). . . . **Having avoided a full and open discussion of the question of the objective humanity of the unborn child, the Supreme Court ruled, on moral grounds, that life** *effectively* **begins under the law no earlier than viability "because the fetus then presumably has the capability of** *meaningful* **life outside the mother's womb"** (*Wade*, p. 48).[16]

In this there is an attempt by judicial decree to change nature: that is, that before the viability of the fetus there is no human life.

The affirmation would be laughable were it not so tragic. This decree has sanctioned the legal extermination of millions of unborn children.

Viability

In current American law, then, human life does not begin before viability. But what is viability? "It is that stage of fetal development when the baby is 'potentially able to live outside the mother's womb [that is, can survive], albeit with artificial help' " (*Roe v. Wade*, p. 45).[17]

Could viability be a valid condition for determining the legal existence of human life?

It is known that the embryo cannot normally survive outside the womb, although its life is totally distinct from that of the mother. The vital principle which makes it grow comes not from the mother, but rather is its own independent impulse.

In view of this indisputable biological fact, when does an embryo become *viable*?

The expression *viable* is ambiguous. If by *viability* we understand the capacity to continue developing independently out-side the womb, then, based on the most elementary experience, we are forced to conclude that even children born at the end of a nine month pregnancy and having a normal birth weight are not viable. Without the constant care of the mother or another person they would die in a short time. This dependency ex-tends into the early infancy of children and gradually diminish-es without ever disappearing entirely in the later years.

Applied to embryonic life, what has *viability* come to mean? In the last century, premature babies before the seventh month were generally doomed to death because of the lack of adequate technical means for keeping them alive. For already three decades, medical progress has made it possible to sus-tain babies born after the thirtieth week. Today it is possible to save a baby born after the twentieth week. Scientists are now trying to develop an artificial placenta which would make ten-week-old embryos viable.

Could such relative conditions, like a kind of magic wand, serve as a basis for determining the moment when a human life begins to exist?

Viable or not, the human life is the same. What has changed are the technical means for protecting and improving human gestation. "Viability is a measure of the sophistication of the life support systems around the baby; it does not measure the humanness or aliveness of the baby himself or herself."[18]

From the philosophical point of view, the argument of via-bility confuses physical independence with ontological inde-pendence. A human individual always has ontological inde-pendence, although its physical independence varies with the different phases and circumstances of its biological life.

A Right to Life? Why Not?

Adopting this criteria, the U.S. Supreme Court came to the following conclusion: "The state's interest in unborn life is not sufficiently compelling to permit regulation of abortion before viability."[19]

What is the social consequence of such an attitude? "The Supreme Court, by denying the right to life to the unborn child, has rent the fabric of human law whereby the inherent worth of every man is recognized."[20]

The inviolable right to life of every innocent human individual constitutes one of the fundamental rights of civil society and of its juridical order. From the moment a positive law deprives a category of human beings—the most innocent among them—of legal protection, the state of law is threatened at its very foundation.

The frightening aspect of using viability as a dimension of someone's right to life is quickly apparent when we consider that, by this standard, a newborn baby or a child of any age with a handicap is also not "viable." By the above criterion, the senile old person rendered incompetent by a stroke, the completely psychotic individual, or even the quadriplegic war veteran is not "viable," since they are not capable of independent existence. Some of these persons also do not have mental "viability." To make a judgment of an unborn child's right to live or not in our society by his mental or physical competence, rather than merely by the fact that he is human and alive, brings only too close the state's determination of a person's right to continued life as measured by one's mental or physical competence—or whatever the current price tag is.[21]

The fruit of human generation, from the first moment of its existence, demands an unconditional respect due to every human being. Why?

First, because a human embryo from the first moment of its conception is a human individual, and as such, possesses rights, even if it does not have the capacity to exercise them.

Second, because:

> There is precisely a certain number of rights which society is not in a position to grant since these rights precede society; but society has the function to preserve and to enforce them. These are the greater part of those which are today called "human rights" and which our age boasts of having formulated.

> The first right of the human person is his life. He has other goods and some are more precious, but this one is fundamental—the condition of all the others. Hence it must be protected above all others. It does not belong to society, nor does it belong to public authority in any form to recognize this right for some and not for others: all discrimination is evil, whether it be founded on race, sex, color or religion. It is not recognition by another that constitutes this right. This right is antecedent to its recognition; it demands recognition and it is strictly unjust to refuse it.

> Any discrimination based on the various stages of life is no more justified than any other discrimination. The right to life remains complete in an old person, even one greatly weakened, it is not lost by one who is incurably sick. The right to life is no less to be respected in the small infant just born than in the mature person. In reality, respect for human life is called for from the time that the process of generation begins. From the time

that the ovum is fertilized, a life is begun which is neither that of the father nor of the mother; it is rather the life of a new human being with its own growth. It would never be made human if it were not human already.[22]

Legal Schizophrenia

Although the Supreme Court did not find sufficient motives to protect human embryonic life, our laws do, however, recognize other rights of the unborn, such as the right of inheritance, the right of legal representation, and so on.

The opinion of the Supreme Court removing all legal protection for the unborn child is regressive. ... If the unborn child can inherit, be compensated for pre-natal injuries, can be represented by a guardian, can have his right to continued existence preferred even to the right of the mother to the free exercise of her religion as in blood transfusion cases, and enjoy other such rights, then the law would be schizophrenic to allow the unlimited destruction of that child.[23]

Why is this contradiction in our laws not corrected? What is the reason for this inconsistency?

The Right to Privacy

The legalization of abortion is based on the constitutional "right to privacy," according to which the decision to interrupt a pregnancy is a private matter like sex, family, and religion. Since the decision to obtain an abortion is something very intimate and private, then, the government should not interfere in the matter.

In *Roe v. Wade*, the Supreme Court first declared that one of the "liberties" constitutionally protected against state infringement by the Fourteenth Amendment is the

right to privacy which "encompasses a woman's decision whether or not to terminate her pregnancy." Finding this to be a "fundamental" constitutional right, the Court declared that state laws infringing upon this right cannot be sustained unless they are necessary to effectuate a compelling state interest.[24]

In simple words, this argument could be expressed as follows: "Well, if abortion is against your private moral or religious beliefs, do not have one. But do not try to impose your morality on a woman who wants to have one. She has the right to choose what's best for her in so private a matter. To deny her this right would be to deny her the right of control over her own body."[25]

Marian Faux, a pro-abortion advocate states:

Slightly more than 50 percent of Americans believe the abortion decision is up to the individual woman. It is the only view, I believe, that offers any real relief to an otherwise irresoluble dilemma. Each person can make a decision based on his or her personal beliefs and conscience. No one is forced to have an abortion; no one is forced not to have one.[26]

Analyzing the basis of this argument, we find the following logical consequences:

A decision is private and intimate to the degree that it refers only to the interests of the one who decides. When, however, it involves the interests of others and the rights of third parties, it can no longer be considered *private*, but rather *representative* or *delegated*.

Now, no one can delegate to another the right to decide his own life, because life is not delegated but, rather, lived.

The legitimate rights which a woman has over her own body

end where the body of another—in this case, her preborn child—begins. No one, alleging privacy, can trespass these bounds and trample upon the rights of another. This would extend the limits of privacy at the expense of another's rights.[27]

Just as it would be absurd to condone child abuse by the parents on the grounds that it is a private matter, it is absurd to say that a woman can decide with her doctor if her child should live or die.[28]

To destroy the individuality of someone in the name of the "right to privacy" is to destroy the foundation of privacy's reason for being. Now, this is not the exercise of the "right to privacy," but an act of sheer private absolutism!

Consequently, the government should intervene to protect the right to life of the unborn threatened by the unilateral decision of one of the parties: his mother.

"Back Alley" Abortions

But some pro-abortionists will object that abortions will continue to be performed even if the government outlaws them. They will go underground and will be performed secretly. Wealthy women will be able to purchase abortion services in sophisticated clandestine clinics while, on the other hand, the poor will be forced to resort to "coat hanger abortions" in back alleys and basements without any of the safeguards of modern medicine.

Besides being an unforgivable discrimination against the poor, this prohibition would bring about a dramatic climb in mortalities.

In short, the state should not legislate on matters where the law will not be followed.

But if this were elevated to a principle of law, where would it lead?

In the words of the Willkes:

> **Did you know that more than 1,000,000 cars were stolen in the U.S. last year? Surely, this can't be stopped. Therefore, why not make it legal to steal cars? How many banks were robbed? That is a dangerous occupation. People get killed stealing cars and robbing banks. We'll never be able to stop all car stealing and bank robberies, true? Then, let's legalize car stealing and bank robbing to save those lives.**
>
> **Since when is it possible to eliminate evil by legalizing it?**[29]

Another example: would legalizing the consumption of drugs be the solution to the problem of drug trafficking? One could also find a discrimination against the poor in this example, because they do not have the same access to this deadly market as the wealthy do. Drugs, being illegal, are expensive. In the name of equality, therefore, should not heroin, cocaine, and other drugs be legalized so as to be within reach of all, regardless of income?

On the other hand, who can guarantee that legalization of abortion eliminates clandestine abortions? The affirmation is superficial and inconsistent. It is based on an erroneous premise and on false statistics.

In fact, the statistics prove unequivocally that in the countries where abortions were legalized in order to prevent clandestine abortion, not only did the number of procured abortions increase progressively, but also the incidence of clandestine abortions did not diminish.[30]

This is not surprising, since the same psychological reasons lead a woman to seek either legal or illegal abortion. There will always be women who have motives to hide the fact that they are pregnant, as, for example, when the pregnancy is the result of adultery. Neither a public hospital nor a private clinic is always able to provide adequate anonymity for covering up this sort of crime. (Interestingly, many former "back alley" abortionists hung out their shingles when abortion was legalized. Moving the abortion mill from the back alley to Main Street is not genuine human progress.)

Those who practice abortion are not only determined not to follow one objective moral law (not to commit murder), but they therewith have the propensity to violate all other moral laws which they do not like. Favoring this propensity by means of legislation, in order that it may become manifest and generalized, opens the door for the complete destruction of the social and legal order of a country.

On the other hand, it is known that the legalization of abortion has significantly stimulated the growth of secret businesses, such as specialists in home abortions. Moreover, the increasing demand has led to a gradual decrease in the quality of the service offered, since the more quickly the abortions are done the greater the profit will be for the feticide business.

The legalization of abortion has, thus, led to more deaths than when they were done illegally. "Legal abortion deaths of mothers," write the Willkes, "have replaced the illegal ones. If abortion were outlawed, we would see a 90% reduction in abortions performed and probably a similar reduction in abortion deaths."[31]

David Reardon concluded:

In the simplest of terms, legalization has improved the odds that an individual will survive an abortion, but the astronomical increase in the number of abortions performed means that more women are dying. *The percentage chance of survival is improved, but the absolute number of those who suffer has increased!*

... it seems clear that the number of women dying and suffering from physical complications alone far exceeds the number who would have suffered similarly if abortion had remained illegal. Rather than reducing the pain and suffering of women, legalization of abortion has increased it by exposing many more women to its inherent risks. The only difference is that now the pain and suffering can be antiseptically ignored because it is "legal." Pro-abortionists go to great lengths to point out the reduced percentage chance of complications, but they consistently ignore the increase in the absolute total of complications.

In brief, what has been gained is not fewer deaths among aborted women, but fewer births. . . . Legalization clearly has not improved the overall health and welfare of American women. Instead, legalization of abortion has only made it easier to pressure women into taking the risk and paying the price.[32]

Discrimination Against Poor Women?

The argument is childish. It ignores the simple and notorious fact that the well-to-do are more favorable to abortion than the poor. One only need attend a "pro-choice" rally to see this.[33]

Contrary to what the heralds of abortion would have us believe, the poorer classes are more inclined to have children than are the rich.

For this reason, birth control is a phenomenon much more prevalent in the richer classes than in the poorer classes.

A lower birthrate begins everywhere—in ancient Greece and Rome as in modern society—not in the neediest classes, but in the richest, precisely those which could have many children with good living conditions.

Misery is not the principle cause of declining population. Populations with the lowest birthrate are the richest. . . Fertile populations are generally poorer with few demands.[34]

Well-known sex-researcher Dr. Alfred Kinsey, notoriously sympathetic to the pro-abortion cause, admits that abortion has always been relatively uncommon among poor people due to their generally being more accepting of children and, indeed, more likely to consider larger families as the ideal. For this reason, Dr. Kinsey's conclusion is clear: "induced abortion is strongly connected with status-striving." [35]

Therefore, if there is any question of discrimination when it comes to abortion, it is made by pro-abortionists, since to equate a poor woman with a woman favoring abortion is to distinguish her as morally degraded. Poverty was never a cause of moral degradation, whereas wealth sometimes is.

Public Funding for Murder?

Abusing the poor to protect their special interests, abortionists claim that cutting off taxpayer funding of abortion would increase mortality among low-income women, who cannot afford professional abortion services.

This feeling of compassion for the poor mother is all the

more surprising since it comes from those who favor the mass killing of millions of human beings. They pretend to protect the poor mother by profiting from the death of her children!

If unborn children are living human beings just like the poor mother, in the name of what principle can one be killed in order, supposedly, to protect the other?

If the fetuses were only simple things to the point that they are considered disposable, how can abortionists pretend to feel such pity on account of the death of poor women, since they too would only be leading poor meaningless lives?

Those who present themselves as being so compassionate for the poor, defending the idea that life must be dignified for everyone, are the same ones who promote the mass extermination of the unborn. What right do they have, on the claim of saving someone from a meaningless existence, to the lives of the children of the poor?

"The humanity of homicide is anything except a human humanity, in the same way that a mother who asks for an abortion is anything but a mother!"[36]

Public money should, therefore, favor life, never death; the economically disadvantaged and never "humanicides."

With Pope John Paul II, we say:

Against the pessimism and selfishness which cast a shadow over the world, the Church stands for life: In each human life she sees the splendor of that "yes," that "amen," who is Christ himself. To the "no" which assails and afflicts the world, she replies with this living "yes," thus defending the human person and the world from all who plot against and harm life.[37]

Not Knowing How to Choose,
They Will Not Know How to Be Mothers

Surrounded on all sides by arguments, abortionists neverthe-less strive to find a way out by using false motives to hide their nihilist hypocrisy. Let us take a quick look at some of them:

"If a woman is not considered mature enough to choose an abortion, how can she be mature enough to be a mother?"

For a pregnant woman, to be a mother is not an option, but a reality. For the same reason that no one can choose the par-ents he has, so also parents cannot choose which children they will have.

The lack of maturity is no reason for someone to commit a murder. If a teenager conceives a child out of wedlock, she cannot remedy one evil by committing another.

No woman knows how to be a mother, until she becomes one. With each child a mother has, her experience in caring for children deepens. To expect to achieve maturity in motherhood with-out having children is

Who would dare say that to become a good sky diver one should first jump without a parachute?

akin to hoping to become an experienced sky diver without a parachute.

At the same time, it often happens that abortionist mothers mistreat their "wanted children." Since the *Roe v. Wade* decision, child abuse has grown proportionally with the rise in the number of legal abortions. Psychiatrist Philip Ney states that the New York Central Registry, for example, reported an 18-20 percent annual increase in incidences of battered children from 1974 to 1975, which, according to estimates, translates into some 1,500,000 battered children in the following decade, "resulting in 50,000 deaths and 300,000 permanently injured children in the United States."[38]

Teenage Pregnancy and the Right to Choose

"Obliging a pregnant teenager to give birth to her child"—so goes another pro-abortion argument—"is to punish her by denying her self-respect and impeding the realization of her full potential in life. Because of this, she should have the option of choosing whether or not to interrupt her pregnancy."

No one learns anything useful by committing a crime. On the contrary, the first fruit of an evil action is a lie; in general, the criminal tries to deny the evil of the act that he has committed. When that fails, he tries to justify it. In both cases, by always lying to himself, he becomes degraded in his own eyes and destroys his prospects in life.

A study promoted by Women Exploited by Abortion (WEBA) revealed interesting data corroborating this: Right after having procured an abortion, more than 70 percent of the interviewed women refused to admit having erred by choosing to kill their unborn child. Others came to recognize their guilt only some months after the abortion, while the majority did so only after more than ten years had gone by.

In the same study:

> **Nearly one-third of the women surveyed described themselves as drinking more heavily after their abortions, while 15 percent admitted that they became alcoholics. Allowing for overlap, 40 percent said that after their abortions, they began to use or increased their use of drugs. Eleven percent described themselves as having become drug addicts.**[39]

If this happens to adult women, what about teenagers? Would letting an adolescent fall into a situation like this—under the pretext of maintaining an option—not truly be a manifestation of psychological sadism?

Summarizing, this is definitely not a way to learn self-respect, to gain the respect of others, nor to realize the goals she has set for herself.

Are Adolescents Incapable of Being Good Mothers?

"Compared to the children born of adult mothers"—charge the abortionists anew—"the children of adolescents have a greater chance of growing up in poverty, amidst resentment and hatred. Rarely do they receive an adequate education, and they frequently become victims of abuse."

Children born of adolescents can be given to dedicated adoptive parents. The facts demonstrate that there are more prospective parents waiting to adopt than there are teenage mothers, which should make it easy to find a solution to the problem.

In the United States alone, more than 2,000,000 requests to adopt a child remain unfulfilled each year. According to the

National Committee on Adoption, only sixty-five thousand children are available for adoption annually.[40] It is evident, therefore, that children born of teenage mothers would have a chance of being well taken care of.

Nevertheless, some leaders of the abortion movement are among those who are critical of the adoption system itself, alleging that it takes away the rights a mother has over the child.

However, every right over a human being necessarily implies a reciprocal: the mother has rights over the child and vice versa, that is, the child also has the right to be treated well by the mother, and not only after birth, but from the moment of conception.

But abortionists deny the unborn this right while hypocritically defending the rights of mothers against the adoption system which seeks to eliminate abortions.

To show even more clearly the absurdity of the pro-choice argument, it suffices to mention the results of a study based on 375,000 children in the United States: At thirty years of age, children born of adolescent mothers were earning on average just as much as children born of adult mothers.[41]

What reliability, then, do these dire predictions of abortionists about the children of teenage mothers really have?

Without doubt, one must take into account that minors are not fully responsible. For this same reason, they, more than anyone else, should be assisted by their parents in order to avoid actions that will be detrimental to their welfare. To the extent that the law hinders abortions, it would also favor the teenage mother, and the parents as well. Young mothers then would not find themselves in need of undertaking a risky and infamous venture.

Being Born into a Hostile World

"What is the lesser evil," ask the pharisaical abortionists, "to interrupt a pregnancy or let a child be born into a world never knowing his father, without the warmth and affection of a home, wearing on his forehead the ugly label: 'child of an unwed mother'?"

No one can decide the future of another on the basis of the projections of his own future. We are not the soothsayers of our children's future, but only their parents. This position reveals a superstitious and deterministic attitude that deprives a person of the possibility of making an objective evaluation about a concrete situation.

Once again, why is there no recourse to adoption? Or, why not get married and form a home with conditions for education and for resolving the situation of the illegitimate children?

In any case, the greater evil will always be abortion, not only for the unborn child who is exterminated, but also for the mother who has an abortion.

In this regard, medical research shows that abortion can lead to numerous grave complications besides the notorious danger of death.[42]

Similarly, the Wynn report states:

> **The complications of subsequent pregnancy resulting in children born handicapped in greater or lesser degree could be the most expensive consequence of induced abortion for society and [its] most grievous consequence for the individual and her family.**[43]

How then can one consider as a greater evil the label, "child of an unwed mother"? What happened to the common sense of the person who raised this objection? Perhaps it was the result of the lucubrations of some visionary or sectarian mind that allowed itself to be clouded by some gross passions!

Rape and Incest

Here is a delicate question, one that generally raises strong emotions owing to the dramatization of the case.

"A woman forced to give birth to a child conceived because of rape or incest is violated twice: first, by the criminal, and then by the authoritarian state that would prevent her from having an abortion and force her to bear a child who would be the incarnation of her abuser."

This objection is, however, based on two absurdities:

In the first place, a child is the "incarnation of a criminal" only in the deformed minds of other potential criminals. It is absolutely unjust that a newly conceived child who is entirely innocent should be punished with death for a crime committed by his father.

The state, in the case at hand, has a grave obligation to help the victims of sexual violence, especially since, from the legal and sociological point of view, the number of effective pregnancies resulting from rape and incest is statistically very small.

In the second place, women in such circumstances are victims not of pregnancy but of rape or incest. Pregnancy can never be considered a crime, unless of course the abortionists are adherents of Manichaeanism or the Albigensian sect of the Middle Ages.

If not even a convicted rapist is sentenced to death for his horrendous crime, how can an innocent child resulting from rape or incest be sentenced to capital punishment?

This death sentence, coldly handed down by those who say they are opposed to an authoritarian state, in reality proves the impudence of those who formulated the objection.

What is really necessary is not that abortion be encouraged, but rather that rape and incest be stopped.

All this being said, let us now take a look at some of the victims of rape or incest. In a paper published in 1979, medical researcher and rape-victim counselor Sandra Mahkorn detailed the results of her study of thirty-seven rape victims who became pregnant. She found that twenty-eight decided to carry their pregnancy to term and five chose abortion; it was not possible to determine what happened to the remaining four.

Of the twenty-eight who chose to continue their pregnancies, seventeen chose adoption, three chose to raise the child themselves, while it was not possible to determine what the other eight decided to do. When questioned about the reasons that prompted these rape victims to continue the pregnancy rather than kill their child through abortion, the most frequently cited reason was that this would be nothing less than another act of violence and immorality and a veritable murder.[44]

Faced with this, the objection loses all its sentimental impact and gives way to balance and reflection.

We recall the words of Pope John Paul II:

When a child is described as a burden or is looked

**upon only as a means to satisfy an emotional need, we
will stand up and insist that every child is a unique and
unrepeatable gift of God, with the right to a loving and
united family.**[45]

Avoiding the Cruelty of a Deformed Being

Another objection loaded with hypocritical sentimentality
may be stated as: "It's cruel to let a child be born that is
deformed or infected with a grave disease such as AIDS. It
would be subject, without justification, to unspeakable suffer-
ings and unhappiness."

Apparently, the child has become the object of pity of the
abortionists. . . . However, precisely because they love it so
much, they want to kill it!

The legitimacy or illegitimacy of induced abortion is not
dependent on the level of misfortune or dramatic circumstances that might strike the mother or her child. Everyone
knows that each pregnancy entails a margin of risk that the
child will be born with a defect of some kind resulting from
heredity, transmission of a grave disease during pregnancy,
or the birth itself.

If, because of this inherent risk, parents had the right to suppress the life of the unborn, then the right to abortion would
exist for any pregnancy whatsoever. This is evidently an
absurdity.

On the other hand, a Christian knows that the soul is much
more valuable than the body and, because of this, the soul is
capable, with the help of divine grace, of overcoming bodily
miseries no matter how bad they may be. History very moving-
ly narrates the stories of Helen Keller and King Baldwin IV, the

Leper, for example.

Professor Jerome Lejeune recounts, in this regard, the following story he heard from a fellow geneticist:

> **Many years ago, my father was a Jewish physician in Braunau, Austria. On one particular day, two babies had been delivered by one of his colleagues. One was a fine, healthy boy with a strong cry. His parents were extremely proud and happy. The other was a little girl, but her parents were extremely sad, for she was a Mongoloid baby. I followed them both for almost fifty years. The girl grew up, living at home, and was finally destined to be the one who nursed her mother through a very long and lingering illness after a stroke. I do not remember her name. I do, however, remember the boy's name. He died in a bunker in Berlin. His name was Adolf Hitler.**[46]

And Pedro-Juan Viladrich narrates this story:

> **After Monod had defended in a lecture the rationale of abortion in cases in which the birth of a deformed child was foreseeable, one of his assistants posed the following problem to him:**
>
> **"If you knew that a father with syphilis and a mother with tuberculosis had had four children, of which the first was born blind, the second died at birth, the third was a deaf-mute, and the fourth had tuberculosis, what would you do when the mother became pregnant for the fifth time?"**
>
> **Monod affirmed categorically: "I would interrupt the pregnancy!"**
>
> **His questioner retorted: "Then you would have killed Beethoven...."**[47]

The Need for Contraception

"Contraception," the antilife crowd solemnly proclaims, "would bring the abortion nightmare to an end and, therefore, the state should promote birth control. From early on, adolescents should be taught how to make effective use of the different methods of contraception. This in turn would solve the difficult problem of unwanted pregnancies."

Contraception essentially destroys at the very root the will to have children. This being so, when it fails, persons who practice it resort to abortion without qualms, while those who do not are also less likely to resort to abortion.

Hence, contraception leads to more abortions rather than eliminating them.

In this regard, Malcolm Potts, the former medical director of the International Planned Parenthood Federation, foresaw in 1973: "As people turn to contraception, there will be a rise, not a fall, in the abortion rate."[48]

In similar terms, Dr. Wanda Poltawska, psychiatrist and director of the Marriage and Family Institute, which has its headquarters in Krakow, Poland, wrote:

> **Paradoxically, however, as contraception was given the "green light" the number of abortions also increased. It seemed obvious that wherever the contraceptive mentality prevailed, abortion would be the logical outcome of contraceptive failure. Therefore, in countries that admitted contraception for general use, the increasing number of abortions compelled authorities to make them legal.**[49]

Viladrich writes,

> **Human life and its origin are naturally linked to the**

sexual behavior of the human couple. When the couple, for whatever reasons, depreciates life, they trivialize sexual relations; and when they trivialize sexual relations, they also depreciate human life.[50]

And well did Pope Paul VI affirm,

It is disquieting to verify in this field a type of fatalism that takes possession even of those in positions of responsibility. Such a feeling leads sometimes to Malthusian solutions, exalted by an active propaganda in favor of contraception and abortion. [51]

A Contradiction Within the Catholic Church?

Some abortionists, demonstrating total ignorance of ecclesiastical history, contend: "It was not until the pontificate of Pius IX that abortion was deemed homicide from the moment of conception. Prior to that time, it was considered so only after the soul had been created, which happened sometime after conception. Now, if for so many centuries the Church thought one way and then changed her way of thinking, is not there a point of contradiction here which frees one's conscience?"

The Catholic Church has always condemned abortion as a very grave crime comparable to murder.

In the authoritative words of the Sacred Congregation for the Doctrine of the Faith:

The tradition of the Church has always held that human life must be protected and favoured from the beginning, just as at the various stages of its development. Opposing the morals of the Greco-Roman world, the Church of the first centuries insisted on

the difference that exists on this point between those morals and Christian morals. In the Didache it is clearly said: "You shall not kill by abortion the fruit of the womb and you shall not murder the infant already born." Athenagoras emphasizes that Christians consider as murderers those women who take medicines to procure an abortion; he condemns the killers of children, including those still living in their mother's womb, "where they are already the object of the care of divine Providence." Tertullian did not always perhaps use the same language; he nevertheless clearly affirms the essential principle: "To prevent birth is anticipated murder; it makes little difference whether one destroys a life already born or does away with it in its nascent stage. The one who will be a man is already one."

In the course of history, the Fathers of the Church, her Pastors and her Doctors have taught the same doctrine—the various opinions on the infusion of the spiritual soul did not introduce any doubt about the illicitness of abortion. It is true that in the Middle Ages, when the opinion was generally held that the spiritual soul was not present until after the first few weeks, a distinction was made in the evaluation of the sin and the gravity of penal sanctions. Excellent authors allowed for this first period more lenient case solutions which they rejected for following periods. But it was never denied at the time that procured abortion, even during the first days, was [an] objectively grave fault. This condemnation was in fact unanimous. Among the many documents it is sufficient to recall certain ones. The first Council of Mainz in 847 reconsiders the penalties against abortion which had been established by preceding Councils. It decided that the most rigorous penance would be imposed "on women who procure the elimination of the fruit conceived in their womb." The Decree of Gratian reports the following words of Pope Stephen V: "That person is a murderer who causes to perish by abortion what has been conceived." Saint Thomas, the Common Doctor of the Church, teaches that abortion is a grave sin against the natural law. At the time of the Renaissance Pope Sixtus V condemned abortion with the greatest severity. A century later, Innocent XI rejected the propositions of certain lax canonists who sought to excuse an abortion procured before the moment accepted by some as the moment of the spiritual animation of the new being. In our days the recent Roman Pontiffs have proclaimed the same doctrine with the greatest clarity. Pius XI explicitly answered the most serious objections. Pius XII clearly excluded all direct abortion, that is, abortion which is either an end or a means. John XXIII recalled the teaching of the Fathers on the sacred character of life "which from its beginning demands the action of God the Creator." Most recently, the Second Vatican Council, presided over by Paul VI, has most severely condemned abortion: "Life must be safeguarded with extreme care from conception; abortion and infanticide are abominable crimes." The same Paul VI, speaking on this subject on many occasions, has not been afraid to declare that this teaching of the Church "has not changed and is unchangeable."[52]

— NOTES —

1. Cf. Dr. Johann B. Weiss, *Los Hebreos; Los Fenicios: Sus Viajes y Colonias*, vol. 3 of *Historia Universal* (Barcelona: La Educación, 1937), pp. 904-905.

2. Pedro-Juan Viladrich, *Aborto e Sociedade Permissiva* (São Paulo: Quadrante, Sociedade de Publicações Culturais, 1987), p. 74.

3. Josef Pieper, *Justice* (New York: Pantheon, 1955), pp. 21-22.

4. In the United States from 1973 to 1990, with data supplied by the Alan Guttmacher Institute, no less than 26,214,015 unborn children were exterminated through procured abortion. This represents an average annual increase of one hundred twenty-three percent. (Cf. Stanley K. Henshaw, et al., "Abortion Services in the United States, 1987 and 1988," *Family Planning Perspectives*, vol. 22, no. 3, May-June 1990, p. 103.)

5. Cf. Viladrich, op. cit., pp. 12-14.

6. Cf. *Roe v. Wade*, 410 U.S. 158 (1973).

7. Cf. *Sierra Club v. Morton*, 405 U.S. 741-752 (1971).

8. The abortionist Dr. Howard I. Diamond, went so far as to say, "I feel sorry for a starving cat. A fetus that nobody wants—that's not sad" (in William Brennan, *The Abortion Holocaust: Today's Final Solution* [St. Louis: Landmark Press, 1983], pp. 99 and 102).

9. "In the landmark Dred Scott decision [March 6, 1857] the court ruled once and for all that black people were not legal 'persons' according to the U.S. Constitution. A slave was the property of the owner and could be bought and sold, used, or even killed by the owner at the owner's discretion" (Dr. and Mrs. John C. Willke, *Abortion: Questions & Answers*, [Cincinnati: Hayes Publishing Company, Inc., 1985], p. 17).

10. "In a speech in May 1923, Adolf Hitler asserted: 'The Jews are undoubtedly a race, but not human'" (in Brennan, op. cit., p. 96).

11. Edward C. Freiling, Ph.D., *The Position of Modern Science on the Beginning of Human Life* and Thomas L. Johnson, Ph.D., *Why a Human Embryo or Fetus Is Not a Parasite* (Thaxton, Va.: Sun Life, Greystone, n.d.), p. 8.

12. In *The Custody Dispute over Seven Human Embryos: The Testimony of Professor Jerome Lejeune, M.D., Ph.D.* (Annandale, Va.: Center for Law and Religious Freedom, 1991), p. 17.

   The only scientific objection worthy of note against the fact that human life begins at fertilization is in the case of the development of identical twins (monozygotic twins), that is, when one fertilized egg gives rise to two human lives. From whence arises the question: at what moment was there a differentiation between the human lives? At what moment do they become distinct?

   If a fertilized egg can produce more than one human life, through a process which is still not entirely understood scientifically, that does not mean that before the division there was not already a human life distinct from that of the mother.

   In any case, this is inconsequential for the central problem we are dealing with: Impeding the development of a group of cells, whether they go on to form one or two lives, is, fundamentally, the taking of human life!

13. In brilliant testimony before the Court of Maryville, Tennessee, Professor Jerome Lejeune made the following affirmations based on the most recent biological data, which proves in an admirable way that a specifically human life begins at the moment when the mother's egg is fertilized:

   "The very young human being, just after fertilization, after it has split in two cells and then in three cells because curiously we do not split ourselves in two, four, eight and continue like that, no, at the beginning we don't do that. . . . After that stage of three cells, it starts again, it comes to four, and it continues by multiples of two.

   "What could be the meaning? . . .

   "It's probably at that time that a message goes from one cell to the two other cells, comes back to the first one and suddenly realizes we are not a population of cells. We are bound to be an individual. That is individualization, that makes the difference between a population of cells which is just a tissue culture and an individual which will build himself according to his own rule, is demonstrated at the three cells stage, that is very soon after fertilization has occurred. . . .

". . . since the last two years, we know that the uniqueness of the early human being I was talking [about] at the beginning, which was a statistical certainty (but an inference of all we knew about the frequency of the genes, about the difference between individuals) is now an experimentally demonstrated fact. That has been discovered less than two years ago by Jeffreys in England, the remarkable manipulator of DNA. And Jeffreys invented that he could select a little piece of DNA, of which he could manufacture a lot of it, which is specific of some message in our chromosomes. It is repeated a lot of times in many different chromosomes and which is probably a regulation system. Some indication to do something or do another thing, but not a kitchen recipe, but a precision about what to do. . . .

". . . there are so many of those little genes and there are so many little changes in them. . . . it looks exactly like the bar code that you have probably seen in the supermarket, that is, small lines of different breadth and different distance from each other. . . .

"It's exactly what it tells us when we look at the DNA bar code, and we detect every individual is different from the next one by its own bar code. And that is not any longer a demonstration by statistical reasoning. So many investigations have been made that we know now that looking at the bar code with his Jeffreys system, the probability that you will find it identical in another person is less than one in a billion. So it's not any longer a theory that each of us is unique. It's now a demonstration as simple as a bar code in the supermarket. It does not tell you the price of human life, it has a difference with a supermarket" (in *The Custody Dispute over Seven Human Embryos: The Testimony of Professor Jerome Lejeune, M.D., Ph.D.*, pp. 54-56).

14. Dr. William A. Liley, *A Case Against Abortion*, Liberal Studies, Whitcombe & Tombs, Ltd., 1971, in Dr. and Mrs. Willke, op. cit., pp. 51-52.

15. The Sacred Congregation for the Doctrine of the Faith, "Instruction on Respect for Human Life in Its Origin and on the Dignity of Procreation," February 22, 1987, no. 5, *Origins*, vol. 16, no. 40, March 19, 1987, p. 701.

16. National Conference of Catholic Bishops, "Testimony on Constitutional Amendment Protecting Unborn Human Life Before the Sub-Committee on Constitutional Amendments of the Senate Committee on the Judiciary," March 7, 1974, II.

    See also the lucid open letter from the noted fetologist, Dr. Landrum B. Shettles, M.D., to the U.S. Supreme Court which was published in the *New York Times* of February 14, 1973.

    In Fr. Rosario Thomas, comp., *The Philosophy of Life: The Pope and the Right to Life* (Pro Fratribus Press, 1989), pp. 248 and 252.

17. Dr. and Mrs. Willke, op. cit., p. 56.

18. Ibid.

19. James Bopp, Jr., "A Human Life Amendment," in Jeff Lane Hensley, ed., *The Zero People* (Ann Arbor, Mich.: Servant Books, 1983), p. 239.

    The U.S. Supreme Court ruled in 1979 that: "viability is what the doctor says it is" (*Colautti v. Franklin*, 429 U.S. 379, 1979).

    In this manner, the doctor has legally taken on the status of a lord over the life of another, in the same way that the *pater familias* (the father of the household) in ancient times enjoyed the legal prerogative of deciding the life or death of his dependents. . . .

20. National Conference of Catholic Bishops, op. cit., II, in Fr. Rosario Thomas, op. cit., p. 252.

    In his allocution of December 18, 1987, Pope John Paul II expressed himself on this fundamental point:

    "The unconditional respect for the right to life of the human person already conceived and not yet born is one of the pillars upon which every civil society supports itself. When a State makes its institutions available so that someone can translate into act the will to suppress the conceived child, it renounces one of its primary duties and its very dignity as a State.

"Saint Thomas Aquinas, one of the great masters of the European conscience, teaches that civil law 'has the force of law in the measure of its justice.' This justice—as the Angelic Doctor immediately explains—is founded upon the natural law itself, such that a law not conforming to it 'is not a law, but the corruption of the law.' "

21. Dr. and Mrs. Willke, op. cit., p. 57.

22. The Sacred Congregation for the Doctrine of the Faith, "On Procured Abortion," November 18, 1974, nos. 10-13, *Social Justice Review*, November 1974, p. 207.

23. National Conference of Catholic Bishops, op. cit., III, in Fr. Rosario Thomas, op. cit., p. 254.

24. Bopp, op. cit., in Hensley, op. cit., p. 238.

25. "In many countries the public authorities which resist the liberalization of abortion laws are the object of powerful pressures aimed at leading them to this goal. This, it is said, would violate no one's conscience, for each individual would be left free to follow his own opinion, while being prevented from imposing it on others. Ethical pluralism is claimed to be a normal consequence of ideological pluralism. There is, however, a great difference between the one and the other, for action affects the interests of others more quickly than does mere opinion. Moreover, one can never claim freedom of opinion as a pretext for attacking the rights of others, most especially the right to life" (Sacred Congregation for the Doctrine of the Faith, "On Procured Abortion," no. 2, p. 205).

Marian Faux, *Roe v. Wade: The Untold Story of the Landmark Supreme Court Decision That Made Abortion Legal* (New York: New American Library, 1989), p. xi.

In this respect, it is opportune to recall the doctrine of Saint Paul about the rights one has over his own body in matters of reproduction: "The wife hath not power of her own body, but the husband. And in like manner the husband also hath not power of his own body, but the wife" (1 Cor. 7:4).

28. It is interesting to point out the absurdities to which this argument used by abortionists can lead: "Not long ago a man in England, called the 'Yorkshire Ripper,' maintained that he was ordered by God to kill prostitutes. It was, he maintained in court, a matter of conscience," a private matter.

   Cf. John Powell, S.J., *Abortion: The Silent Holocaust* (Allen, Tex.: Argus Communications, 1981), pp. 111-112.

29. Dr. and Mrs. Willke, op. cit., p. 169.

30. Cf. *American Journal of Public Health*, no. 1967; *British Medical Journal*, May, 1970-1972.

   See also the interesting study of Dr. Thomas Hilgers, *Induced Abortion: A Documented Report* (2nd ed., Minnesota Citizens Concerned for Life, 1973, chap. 7), in which he demonstrates that the index of clandestine abortions remained unchanged in eight European countries even after it was legalized.

31. Dr. and Mrs. Willke, op. cit., pp. 165-166.

32. David C. Reardon, *Aborted Women: Silent No More* (Chicago: Loyola University Press, 1987), pp. 292-293.

33. In an interesting study, the sociologist Donald Granberg analyzes the moral and sociopolitical profile of the membership of the major organizations in favor of and against abortion. He found, for example, that the members of the National Abortion Rights Action League (NARAL) generally belong to the wealthier classes, are permissive in their sexual standards, and are commonly agnostics and atheists. (Cf. Donald Granberg, "The Abortion Activists," *Family Planning Perspectives*, July-August 1981, pp. 157-163.)

34. Jacques Leclerq, *La Familia* (Barcelona: Editorial Herder, 1979), p. 213.

35. Paul H. Gebhard, et al., *Pregnancy, Birth and Abortion* (New York:

John Wiley & Sons, 1958), in Germain G. Grisez, *Abortion: The Myths, the Realities, and the Arguments* (New York: Corpus Books, 1972), pp. 52-53.

36. Viladrich, op. cit., p. 44.

37. John Paul II, "The Apostolic Exhortation on the Family," no. 30, *Origins*, vol. 11, nos. 28 and 29, December 24, 1981, p. 447.

38. Cf. Dr. Philip G. Ney, "Infant Abortion and Child Abuse: Cause and Effect," in David Mall and Walter F. Watts, eds., *The Psychological Aspects of Abortion* (Washington, D.C.: University Publications of America, Inc., 1979), p. 25.

39. Reardon, op. cit., p. 23.

40. Cf. Dr. and Mrs. Willke, op. cit., p. 306.

41. Cf. Josefina J. Card, "Long-Term Consequences for Children of Teenage Parents," *Demography*, vol. 18, no. 2, May 1981, pp. 137-156.

42. Among the possible complications arising from abortion, some of the more outstanding are:

"*Immediate*: Intense pain, Punctured uterus, Excessive bleeding, Infection, Parts of baby left inside, Shock/Coma, Damage to other organs, Death

"*Later*: Inability to become pregnant again, Miscarriage/Stillbirths, Tubal pregnancies, Premature births, Pelvic inflammatory disease, Hysterectomy. . . .

"Dr. Anne Speckhard, Ph.D., in her study on Post Abortion Syndrome, found the following effects on women.

"Events Related to Abortion:
- 23% had hallucinations related to the abortion.
- 35% perceived visitation from the aborted child.
- 54% had nightmares related to the abortion.
- 69% experienced feelings of "craziness."

- 73% had flashbacks of abortion experience.
- 81% had a preoccupation with the aborted child" (in *She's a Child Not a "Choice,"* Human Life Alliance of Minnesota, Inc., advertising supplement, Spring 1991) .

43. Margaret and Arthur Wynn, "Some Consequences of Induced Abortion to Children Born Subsequently," Foundation for Education and Research in Child Bearing, London, 1972, p. 6, in Reardon, op. cit., p. 223.

44. Cf. Sandra K. Mahkorn, "Pregnancy and Sexual Assault," in Mall and Watts, op. cit., pp. 58-59.

45. John Paul II, "Love and Respect for Nascent Life," general audience in Paul VI Hall, the Vatican, on January 3, 1979, *L'Osservatore Romano* (English edition), January 8, 1979, p. 3.

46. In Dr. and Mrs. Willke, op. cit., p. 208.

47. Viladrich, op. cit., pp. 60-61.

48. In Andrew Scholberg, "The Abortionists and Planned Parenthood: Familiar Bedfellows," *International Review of Natural Family Planning*, vol. 4, no. 4, Winter 1980, p. 298 in Dr. Donald DeMarco, *The Contraceptive Mentality* (Edmonton, Canada: Life Ethics Centre, 1982), p. 10.

49. Dr. Wanda Poltawska, "The Effect of a Contraceptive Attitude," *International Review of Natural Family Planning*, vol. 4, no. 3, Fall 1980, p. 188 in DeMarco, op. cit., p. 9.

50. Viladrich, op. cit., p. 73.

51. Pope Paul VI, in a general audience of May 14, 1971 in Fr. Rosario Thomas, op. cit., p. 196.

52. The Sacred Congregation for the Doctrine of the Faith, "On Procured Abortion," nos. 6 and 7, p. 206.

— BIBLIOGRAPHY —

Bopp, Jr., James. "A Human Life Amendment." See Hensley.

Brennan, William. *The Abortion Holocaust: Today's Final Solution.* St. Louis: Landmark Press, 1983.

Card, Josefina J. "Long-Term Consequences for Children of Teenage Parents." *Demography,* vol. 18, no. 2, May 1981, pp. 137-156.

DeMarco, Dr. Donald. *The Contraceptive Mentality.* Edmonton, Alberta, Canada: Life Ethics Centre, 1982.

Faux, Marian. *Roe v. Wade: The Untold Story of the Landmark Supreme Court Decision That Made Abortion Legal.* New York: New American Library, 1989.

Freiling, Edward C., Ph.D. *The Position of Modern Science on the Beginning of Human Life* and Thomas L. Johnson, Ph.D., *Why a Human Embryo or Fetus Is Not a Parasite.* Thaxton, Va.: Sun Life, Greystone, n.d.

Gebhard, Paul H.; Pomeroy, Wardell; Martin, Clyde; and Christenson, Cornelia. *Pregnancy, Birth and Abortion.* New York: John Wiley & Sons, 1958.

Granberg, Donald. "The Abortion Activists." *Family Planning Perspectives,* July-August 1981, pp. 157-163.

Grisez, Germain G. *Abortion: The Myths, the Realities, and the Arguments.* New York: Corpus Books, 1972.

Henshaw, Stanley K., et al. "Abortion Services in the United States, 1987 and 1988." *Family Planning Perspectives,* vol. 22, no. 3, May-June 1990, p. 103.

Hensley, Jeff Lane, ed. *The Zero People.* Ann Arbor, Mich.: Servant Books, 1983.

Hilgers, Dr. Thomas. *Induced Abortion: A Documented Report.* 2nd ed. Minnesota Citizens Concerned for Life, 1973.

Human Life Alliance of Minnesota, Inc. *She's a Child Not a "Choice,"* advertising supplement, Spring 1991.

John Paul II. "The Apostolic Exhortation on the Family." *Origins,* vol. 11, nos. 28 and 29, December 24, 1981, pp. 437, 439-448.

———. "Love and Respect for Nascent Life," January 3, 1979. *L'Osservatore Romano* (English edition), January 8, 1979, p. 3.

Leclerq, Jacques. *La Familia.* Barcelona: Editorial Herder, 1979.

Lejeune, Professor Jerome. *The Custody Dispute over Seven Human Embryos: The Testimony of Professor Jerome Lejeune, M.D., Ph.D.* Annandale, Va.: Center for Law and Religious Freedom, 1991.

Liley, Dr. William A. *A Case Against Abortion.* Liberal Studies, Whitcombe & Tombs, Ltd., 1971.

Mahkorn, Sandra K. "Pregnancy and Sexual Assault." See Mall and Watts.

Mall, David, and Watts, Walter F., eds. *The Psychological Aspects of Abortion.* Washington, D.C.: University Publications of America, Inc., 1979.

National Conference of Catholic Bishops. "Testimony on Constitutional Amendment Protecting Unborn Human Life Before the Sub-Committee on Constitutional Amendments of the Senate Committee on the Judiciary," March 7, 1974.

Ney, Dr. Philip G. "Infant Abortion and Child Abuse: Cause and Effect." See Mall and Watts.

Paul VI. General audience of May 14, 1971.

Pieper, Josef. *Justice.* New York: Pantheon, 1955.

Poltawska, Dr. Wanda. "The Effect of a Contraceptive Attitude." *International Review of Natural Family Planning,* vol. 4, no. 3, Fall 1980, p. 188.

Powell, S.J., John. *Abortion: The Silent Holocaust.* Allen, Tex.: Argus Communications, 1981.

Reardon, David C. *Aborted Women: Silent No More.* Chicago: Loyola University Press, 1987.

Sacred Congregation for the Doctrine of the Faith. "On Procured Abortion," November 18, 1974. *Social Justice Review,* November 1974, pp. 205-211.

———. "Instruction on Respect for Human Life in Its Origin and on the Dignity of Procreation," February 22, 1987. *Origins,* vol. 16, no. 40, March 19, 1987, pp. 697, 699-711.

Scholberg, Andrew. "The Abortionists and Planned Parenthood: Familiar Bedfellows." *International Review of Natural Family Planning,* vol. 4, no. 4, Winter 1980, pp. 298-308.

Thomas, Fr. Rosario, comp. *The Philosophy of Life: The Pope and the Right to Life.* Pro Fratribus Press, 1989.

Viladrich, Pedro-Juan. *Aborto e Sociedade Permissiva.* São Paulo: Quadrante, Sociedade de Publicações Culturais, 1987.

Weiss, Dr. Johann B. *Los Hebreos; Los Fenicios: Sus Viajes y Colonias,* vol. 3 of *Historia Universal.* Barcelona: La Educación, 1937.

Willke, Dr. and Mrs. John C. *Abortion: Questions & Answers.* Cincinnati: Hayes Publishing Company, Inc., 1985.

Wynn, Margaret and Arthur. "Some Consequences of Induced Abortion to Children Born Subsequently." London: Foundation for Education and Research in Child Bearing, 1972.